How Management Is Different in Small Companies

An AMA Management Briefing

Theodore Cohn
Roy A. Lindberg

 American Management Association, Inc.

This Management Briefing has been distributed to all members
enrolled in the General Management Division of the American
Management Association. A limited supply of extra copies is
available at $5.00 a copy for AMA members, $7.50 for non-
members.

International standard book number: 0-8144-2154-7

First printing

Acknowledgments

The authors wish to express their thanks to the following executives whose comments are quoted by name in this briefing. (The affiliations and titles given are those held at the time of interviewing.) These executives were among 32 chosen for interview among questionnaire respondents either because they had managerial experience in both small and large companies or because of the interest stimulated by the answers they gave in filling out the study questionnaire. The unidentified quotations were given by respondents whose company policies or feelings about their comments did not permit them to be credited.

Julian G. Andorka, Director, Market Research, Morton International, Inc., Chicago, Ill.

Seymour A. Baum, Marketing Manager, Consumer Products Division, Colgate-Palmolive Company, Jersey City, N.J.

B. M. Carothers, Executive Vice-President, Union Electric Company, St. Louis, Mo.

David A. Eberly, Vice-President, Warwick Electronics, Inc., Chicago, Ill.

Curtis W. Fritze, Vice-President, Corporate Planning, Control Data Corporation, Minneapolis, Minn.

Fred Grunwald, Production Manager, Crazy Horse Division, Russ Togs, New York, N.Y.

Wallace Hodes, Vice-President, Cormedics, Subsidiary of Corning Glass Works, Hodes Lange Plant, North Bergen, N.J.

Robert L. Koch, President, George Koch & Sons, Inc., Evansville, Ind.

Leon A. Marantz, Chief Executive Officer, The Plessey Airborne Corporation, Hillside, N.J.

Franklin A. Moss, Vice President–Finance, J. I. Kislak, Inc., Newark, N.J.

Peter J. Scott, President, Tanatex Chemical Company Division of Sybron Corporation, Lyndhurst, N.J.

Leo Siebert, General Manager, Mundt Perforated Metals Corporation, Jersey City, N.J.

H. Alan Stein, Vice President, Marketing, Shiman Manufacturing Company, Newark, N.J.

D. W. Vaughn, President, Southern Indiana Electric & Gas Company, Evansville, Ind.

William L. West, President, The Torit Corporation, St. Paul, Minn.

The quotations attributed to Dr. Saul Gellerman were obtained in a phone conversation with him.

Theodore Cohn is the Managing Partner of J. H. Cohn & Company in Newark, New Jersey. He received his B.A. degree from Harvard College in 1943, and an M.A. degree from Columbia University in 1948. In addition, he studied accounting at the New York University Graduate School of Business Administration. He is a Certified Public Accountant in New Jersey and New York.

Mr. Cohn is a former president of the Occupational Center of Essex County, and of the New Jersey Rehabilitation Association, and was Chairman of the Management Advisory Services Committee of the New Jersey Society of CPA's. He also is a member of the Technical Studies Committee of the American Institute of CPA's.

Mr. Cohn is a frequent speaker on management and accounting subjects, and is the author of a number of articles in professional and trade association publications on accounting and management subjects. His memberships include the American Accounting Association, the National Association of Accountants, and the New Jersey and New York State Societies of CPA's.

Roy A. Lindberg is Manager of Management Services with J. H. Cohn & Company in Newark, New Jersey. After graduation from college, he studied at the Columbia University Graduate School.

Mr. Lindberg was a professor of philosophy and psychology at Roanoke College prior to entering industry. He began his consulting career in 1953. Since then he has served clients in many basic industries. His teaching experience in the field of management includes lectureships at Rutgers and Southeastern universities and the graduate schools of City College of New York and Drexel Institute of Technology. He has also participated in the Master's Degree Program of the Martin Company in Baltimore and has given talks on management subjects before groups of the U.S. State Department and the personnel of the International Cooperation Administration. He has conducted a number of courses for the Southern Pacific Company, the Skelly Oil Company, the Public Service Company of Oklahoma, and various other clients. He recently served as a member of The Governor's Management Commission (New Jersey) and guest lecturer for the National Development and Management Foundation of South Africa.

Mr. Lindberg is the author of a number of reports and books in the field of organization, operations auditing, and general management.

Contents

Introduction

The thesis of this survey-backed briefing is that businesses that are very different in size must conduct their affairs in different ways. The authors believe that businesses of varying sizes do not merely happen to conduct their affairs differently (which could be reflections of the personalities involved or of cultural patterns), but must so conduct them if they are to survive.

If this thesis is true, two conclusions seem unavoidable:

1. Small businesses require for survival not only good understanding of management techniques as generally practiced but also thorough knowledge of size-related differences in management practice.

2. Exploitation of size-related opportunities is as important to the small company as is the development of product advantages or operating efficiencies.

Managerial competence in small firms is often seriously diluted by uncritical adherence to the belief that the principles of management are applicable in companies of every size. When this belief extends beyond managerial generalizations of the broadest scope, serious problems often arise.

The generally accepted principles of management are based mainly on the experience of large companies. Management personnel have generally assumed that the ways the big producers of goods or services handle their affairs are the best ways for all businesses. Hence, business administration is primarily a description of the methods that have worked in large concerns and has been remarkably neglectful of the needs and ways of small companies. For these reasons the authors believe that the present body of commonly accepted management knowledge does not sufficiently recognize the uniqueness of small firms.

The idea that small companies should be managed under a set of rules in some ways different from those relevant to large firms is supported by the increasing difficulty small firms are having in earning profits as the technological and competitive pace intensifies. Of course, it has been true for a long time that even when adequately financed and managed, small businesses operate under handicaps in an economy in which big firms play key roles. This fact causes some critics of American society to express growing concern that some companies may have expanded beyond the range of effective control, beyond the capacity to respond to the deepening crises of society.

To truly benefit from what observers of business are advocating these days, it is first necessary to understand something about the differences between large and small companies, their inherent strengths and weaknesses, and the advantages and disadvantages caused by size. Since much has been written about large companies, and much less about small, this Briefing will focus on small companies.

The survey on which this report is in part based was mailed to presidents of small companies (defined for the purposes of this study as having annual sales from $2 million to $10 million) and large companies (defined as those with sales from $80 million to $600 million). In addition to providing information that led to many productive interviews, the survey also produced some interesting statistical comparisons of size-related differences because the respondents in both categories were asked identical questions and were also requested to compare the management methods of large and small companies. The results of the survey are given in the tables in the Appendix.

Conclusions

1. Small and big firms must differ deliberately in many of the ways they administer their businesses.

2. Small firms should focus on achieving managerial excellence; they tend to underestimate the need for and the difficulty in attaining such excellence because of the protections offered by their abilities to live in small markets and to profit from short production runs.

3. Where the small businessman does consciously attend to administration, he tends to adopt the methods and practices used in larger firms rather than to develop techniques and applications that are more specific to his needs. This form of imitation usually brings about operating and procedural inefficiencies. Techniques copied from large firms are, in small companies, more often brought in as unrelated bits of administrative magic than as part of an integrated process.

4. Small companies should not try to skimp on management staff; many of the problems of small businesses can be traced to shortages of top personnel.

5. Planning is the most difficult function to perform well in a small company. Therefore, small companies should take pains to see that the effectiveness of planning is raised to the highest level.

6. The poorest part of the planning job done in small firms is the setting of overall goals. Conceptualizing a firm's mission or goals in terms of externals (markets served or aimed at, product needs identified or to be exploited) is much more difficult for the small company than it is for a large firm, even though it is equally necessary in both. The small firm's financial, production, and marketing limitations force it to deal with more factors in less stable environments than large firms must deal with.

7. Small companies should strive to excel in short-term planning. Detailed planning beyond the clearly seen future can induce rigidities that may largely offset or destroy the advantages of a small firm's innate flexi-bility and maneuverability. The smaller quantities of goods produced, fewer salesmen, lower inventory levels, smaller outlays for advertising and promotion, and similar characteristics of small businesses seldom justify the risks or costs imposed by long-range plans.

8. Nothing a small company does in planning should be allowed to impair, even temporarily, customer services and product customization capabilities (which are critical to survival of the small business).

9. Next to the provision of wanted products, keeping costs low is the most important advantage a small firm can possess. Not having the advantages that stem from high capitalization and commodity markets, the profitability of a small firm rests largely on the tighter control that top management close to operations can exercise over the costs of making the products or providing the services it offers.

10. Small companies should seek to automate data processing as soon as technically and economically feasible. Small companies, which in the past did not have the resources to operate on the basis of the best available knowledge, can now afford the information they need (and have hitherto lacked) to manage their affairs on an informed basis. (For example, product profitability analysis, projections, and decision-making aids are available through time-sharing computer terminals and service bureaus at $25–$100 a month.)

11. The manager in a small company can afford less to be a specialist than his big-company counterpart, but he should not try to be all things to his firm. He must be able to contribute to tight control of costs and key resources and be aware of his firm's progress, but he should rely on others (inside or outside the firm) to perform the tasks for which he is not qualified.

12. An inexpensive, proven method of broadening the basis of key decision making in the small firm is through the formation of a carefully chosen and authoritative board of directors or management (advisory) committee with at least a 40 percent outside membership (nonequity).

13. Small companies cannot always afford to make decisions mainly on the basis of the relevant facts or sound reasoning. At certain times and in certain circumstances, the smaller and more personal environment of a small company requires consensus rather than a decision that is objectively arrived at.

14. Although the small company is a more natural habitat for entrepreneurs than the large company, it offers a poorer environment for the radical individualist. The small company is less hierarchical, systematized, and compartmentalized than the large company and is, therefore, more readily disrupted by persons with deficient interpersonal interests and skills.

15. The skills and personal characteristics of executives exert a more powerful influence on the fortunes of small companies than they do on large, and should weigh heavily in determining the kinds of methods and procedures adopted. Methods and procedures in small firms should be designed not only to offset personal deficiencies but also to utilize strengths.

16. Small companies should seek to employ high-potential (entrepreneurial or otherwise gifted) people by emphasizing the special attractions of small businesses. Current shifts in cultural values increasingly favor working in small firms.

17. Small companies lose employees more often for dollars than do large. Small firms should review compensation against the cost of replacing and training key people and make adjustments as needed to attract and keep effective people.

18. Small companies should look for people skilled in handling a high volume of detail and making varied decisions. Ironically, an increasingly important source of such persons is large business.

19. Growth, when it becomes a self-contained objective, exposes the small company to extraordinary hazards. A high percentage of small companies which make a primary aim of getting bigger, and which succeed in greatly increasing sales volume, lose control over costs and strangle on their growth.

20. Small companies can improve their performance by upgrading the quality of directive elements (plans, policies, procedures, and so forth); the advantages of relatively smaller scales of activities in small firms are often lost by failure to employ methods and tools that can significantly reduce the need for information transference and repetitive decision making.

21. Small firms should not make a fetish of keeping organization as simple as possible; they can often benefit from structural arrangements (for example, centralized purchasing) that in large firms create handicaps which exceed the benefits received.

22. Because the risks of failure of original products is great and can cause more serious losses for small companies than for large companies, small firms should lean more toward evolution than invention in product development.

23. When small firms must risk their future on new products (not externally available), they should aim at radical development; many of the greatest product innovations have come from small firms.

24. Small firms have more problems in creating sales than in managing people. The problems of large firms are more the opposite.

1

Executive Opinions About Size-Related Differences in Management

Management of any enterprise is not simple. Most people recognize the fact that running a small business entails hard work, but tend to overlook the complexity of the job. Unfortunately, this is also true of many executives of small businesses who do not have a clear understanding of the nature and methods of administration, and who are thus prone to make one of two major errors:

1. They tend to meet all problems by working harder, rather than introducing new methods, or
2. They tend, in adopting new ways, to follow slavishly the practices and methods of big business.

For an example of this lack of understanding, consider the president of a $3 million a year service company who at first feared that the only way for his business to expand to $4 million was for him to increase his working day from nine to twelve hours. Subsequently, he changed his concept of work to *what* he did rather than *how much* he did.

Two-thirds of the respondents in the survey said that management is more difficult in large than in small companies. It is understandable that most executives of large companies would feel this way, but surprisingly, 55 percent of the small company managers who responded to the questionnaire think so too. Only 43 percent of them said that management of small companies poses greater problems than management of large firms.

Managers interviewed were overwhelmingly of the opinion that size-related differences do exist, although they did not generally agree on any specific differences, with the possible exception of decision making and financing. Most of the small company managers attributed management problems of their firms to shortages of management personnel, while executives of big companies claimed that their management problems were caused mainly by the greater numbers of people to be managed. The majority of small business managers felt that the problems of small firms stem from external causes, while the great majority of large company managers cited internal difficulties as the source of problems.

Specifically, managers of small companies saw the commitment activities (planning, organizing, and training) as posing special problems for the small company. Executives of large companies considered the compliance functions (directing and controlling) as presenting bigger problems.

Differences Bearing on Administration

In commenting on general differences with administrative implications, Peter J. Scott, president of Tanatex Chemical Company, a division of Sybron Corporation, observed: "Small business is more pragmatic and entrepreneurial; it is oriented toward products and small markets. Big business, on the other hand, is concerned more with continuity of the institution."

The group vice-president of a large company in the surgical/medical field noted a difference in bargaining position: "Small business, in many cases, can get things cheaper. It can wheedle, make deals. It knows where to get help cheaper and faster. It can get many types of consultancy, professional advice and help from suppliers, and often from customers, all in areas that big business has to pay for."

Leon A. Marantz, chief executive officer of The Plessey Airborne Corporation, touched on several factors of size-related differences: "Small business has greater flexibility, faster response time, and much faster decision making capability than big business, because in the latter there is a long line of communication to central headquarters people. The manager in a large firm has to justify [explain] his reasons and back up all his major decisions with detailed information."

Robert L. Koch, president of George Koch & Sons, Inc., a small company, contributed this thought: "Big companies have the advantage in linear activities, that is, in repetitive activities, while small companies excel in nonlinear activities (such as the manufacturing of a custom or unique product)."

Moving toward specific differences, a vice-president of a medium-size Ohio utility said: "Small companies do far less in the way of forward planning than big companies. I do not think this is a flaw. A small company does not need to look so far ahead. The pilot of a tugboat only needs to look ahead a quarter of a mile or so, but the pilot of a 200,000-ton tanker must be able to see ahead five miles or more."

William L. West, president of The Torit Corporation, supported this view from his own experience: "I feel just as removed from operations as a top executive in a large company must feel. Forward planning now has swelled to take a good deal of my time. Small companies tend to plan poorly. Few small companies have any formal planning activity at all."

As a company grows, planning becomes increasingly important, according to Curtis W. Fritze, vice-president of corporate planning for Control Data Corporation: "As Control Data grew we found it necessary to alter administrative processes. Planning, for example, had to be made far more comprehensive and systematic if we were to remain in any sense a compact, integrated operation. We now carry planning down to every supervisor."

In talking about specific differences in company size, the chief executive of a small manufacturing firm doing about $6 million in volume pointed out that the key business ratios differ on the basis of business size, and noted: "I believe overhead has to outgrow sales as a company gets bigger."

Peter Scott agreed with this position and attributed the differences, among other things, to the fact that, "Expense controls are much looser in big business."

Differences in Decision Making

Decision making does not appear to present a problem to either group although most respondents felt that company size often determines what approach is taken. A respondent in a large capital goods manufacturing company located in Pennsylvania believes decision making responds to size differences: "There appears to be a major difference between a large and small company in the way decisions are made. This fits in with the generally observed fact that the decision maker in the small company usually arrives at his decision on the basis of personal knowledge. In the large company the decision maker usually must make his decision on the basis of facts and figures, or recommendations supplied to him by others."

The same executive cited another difference in decision making: "The smaller company cannot afford to make bad decisions. A larger corporation has greater latitude in its capacity to make and recover from major mistakes."

"A big company usually has enough momentum to withstand the inadequacies of its members," reported Dr. Julian Andorka, director of market research for Morton International, Inc., "and by some strange metamorphosis this collective power becomes greater than the sum of the individuals involved—similar to a jury. The group judgment is usually superior to the judgment of its individual members."

The Ohio utilities executive interviewed observed: "The difference I see is that small companies can make decisions far faster. In landing the first lunar module Neil Armstrong had to avoid boulders and was given 20 seconds in which to do it. If a committee had to make a business decision in 20 seconds they'd never be able to do it.

"Now I'm not sure there is a parallel between decision speed and decision quality. I'm inclined to think that the quality of decision making in big companies is probably better."

Another respondent agreed: "Decisions are made faster in small business, but not necessarily better. In big business, decisions are not made as fast or as inexpensively but they are made as well as they are in small business."

Peter Scott agreed in part: "Decision making in big

business is much slower and costlier, but it is no better than in small business. The common denominator of judgment applies to decision making in business of all sizes. In big business, decisions relate to ROA (return on assets) or EPS (earnings per share), neither of which is often considered in small business."

Wallace Hodes, vice-president of a Corning Glass Works subsidiary, described how the decision-making process changes as a company grows: "Small businessmen are more subjective, whereas the businessmen in the large companies are more objective. Some of the roots of the problems of small and large businesses lie in these differences.

"When we were a small company we all worked hard. Everyone pitched in. We were a sharing group and a decisive group. We accomplished things, we got them done. We did not even pass each other in the hall without progressing our affairs. Now that we are part of a large company I am appalled by how much time we have to spend to make decisions and by how much time we spend in meetings.

"Despite these handicaps, however, it seems to me that one advantage of large firms is that they have pretty well attended to the matter of setting up the appellate function. They recognize that some decisions are hard to make, and that the structure must be flexible enough to include a conflict-resolving function. Small companies, because the numbers of functions are necessarily limited, tend not to have an appellate function and thus can have differences of opinion that go on forever."

Julian Andorka agreed in part, saying: "Small business can move faster—the decision-making process is shorter. Small business has a fast reaction to both products and markets. I know of one decision facing a big company that involved $150,000 and took four days to catch up with a vice-president in Europe; a manager in a smaller business would have decided himself. Executives in big business are sometimes reluctant to make decisions because the size of the commitments tends to be much larger absolutely; also, the length of time of the dollar commitment results in conservatism in decision making. Once a decision is made and large dollars have been committed, it is very hard for a big company to change its direction. Accumulated economic worth also makes big businesses reluctant to change. The more people who get involved with any project likely to affect that worth, the more they tend to become a force of inertia."

Mr. Marantz claimed that although top management spends a good deal of time documenting decision making, these formalities do not necessarily lead to any better decisions: "Large business requires more accounting and more detail, which results in higher costs but does not provide additional value. It is a form of bureaucratic protection to avoid criticism."

Financial Differences

Fred Grunwald, production manager, Crazy Horse Division of Russ Togs, pointed out: "One of the major disadvantages of small businesses is their financial limitations. The lack of dollars available to small companies reduces the speed with which they can grow and also makes them more conservative about the risks they will take in order to grow. Another drawback of being small is that major customers can take advantage of you. When you are big, this is not possible."

Seymour A. Baum, marketing manager, Consumer Products Division, Colgate–Palmolive Company, noted: "A major difference is that big business is more concerned with long-range earnings per share while small business is more involved with immediate goals and opportunities. Small firms don't dwell so much on long-term survival and are, therefore, much more opportunistic."

A responding executive of a small company said: "Return on investment is the most important factor in the plans of large firms. Smaller companies are more concerned with marketing position and the growth of technology. As companies grow, return on investment of individual products comes to the fore. The large company often has a plan for growth, both on investment return and earnings per share with a long-range 15 percent compounded curve as a goal."

Dr. Andorka remarked: "Frequently the smaller company follows a bank balance fiscal policy. More often than not it hasn't an adequate financial picture."

Mr. West agreed that small companies are not finance-oriented: "Though a principal advantage of smallness is flexibility, most small companies do a poor job of taking care of their finances."

One of the ways in which the problem of finances becomes especially prominent is when a small company is sold to a larger company. One of the executives interviewed who has experienced this, offered a clear explanation:

"The first step in the integration of a small business into a larger one is the accounting integration. This often becomes a major stumbling block for three reasons. First, budgeting is not considered relevant to the small business. Second, the accounting system of the small business is generally not set up for planning and control purposes. Third, the conservatism of the small business to save income taxes does not agree with the pattern of the larger business, which is trying to be consistent and, in many cases, is also interested in achieving higher profits for earnings-per-share results."

Sources of Funds

Although finance is a common thread that runs through all enterprise, there are several size-related differences between big and small companies that determine their sources of money. We will mention several that have been used by the smaller firm.

1. Private placements through investment bankers are a source of capital for the new company or the one in need of funds to develop or expand. Often this method is used before a public issue, one purpose of which may be to pay out all or part of the private placement investment. Since the investors are generally sophisticated, the small company can obtain investment decisions quickly and develop a useful long-term financial relationship. The investor may take, or feel he is required to take, a significant hand in management to protect his investment and offer experienced financial help.

2. Terms of long-term loans from institutional lenders such as insurance companies are generally shorter and more restrictive to smaller companies. Twelve to fifteen years is the normal outside limit of such unsecured loans to a small company. To the larger company, loans of twenty-five to thirty years are common, and the restrictions are less onerous.

3. Loans from small business investment companies and the Small Business Administration are unique to the smaller company. SBIC loans are usually made at higher than bank interest rates to companies whose bank credit is minimal or has been exhausted. Some part of the company's stock is almost always made available to the SBIC through options, warrants, or convertible features in the debt instrument. The extent of participation in management varies.

SBA funds and guarantees of bank loans have been irregularly available. When the faucet is open, they are desirable because they are offered at low interest rates.

4. A major trade vendor is more likely to give special long terms to a small company than to a financially sound large one. For the small company that has established credibility in satisfying its debts, vendor financing is a useful source of funds.

5. Unfixing fixed costs by converting them to variable costs may make sense to companies of all sizes. For the small company that wants to stay flexible, this can be a high priority financial principle. Leasing rather than purchasing, or purchasing through the use of extended term obligations (particularly in periods of inflation when future payments will be in dollars of lesser value) may preserve working capital. Leasing may also permit strategic changes more readily than purchasing because the emotional commitment to sunk costs is less obvious. Production obsolescence may also be reduced.

Other Size-Related Differences

An interesting observation about size-related differences was made by one large company respondent: "One of the limitations in a big company is the growth pressure. A big company can't spend a significant portion of its efforts on consolidating its present position; it's too busy meeting the growth imperative. A small company, on the other hand, can well (and perhaps must) consolidate its present position before it does anything else."

David A. Eberly, vice-president of Warwick Electronics, Inc., observed: "In the smaller company a man can see his accomplishments; he can carry a job through from an idea to the market. That's a very personal kind of thing. In a large company, on the other hand, a man may only be a part of an idea or a project. He is very seldom allowed to stick with a particular activity until it comes to fruition."

Growth for the smaller company is often like a chronic case of adolescence—some part of the corporate body always seems to be out of joint. The organizational changes required are rarely gently evolutionary. They seem to be more like the random bouncing of a ball off a suddenly encountered wall than a gradual change in direction. Especially difficult is the conceptual reorientation of the manager's own functions as previously handled routine chores become overwhelming in number and require delegation; direct contact with customers and workers is infrequent and the touch and smell of the operation fades; decisions are based on second- or third-hand information and on alternatives filtered through possibly biased subordinates.

No training course can adequately prepare a small company manager for this experience since it is unique to each company. How well the small company manager handles the change in his job becomes crucial to the direction his firm takes.

7

2 Planning

In most organizations effective planning is rare—in the sense of identifying and establishing worthy, attainable objectives and of correctly proportioning, assigning, and programming use of the physical, human, temporal, and economic resources required to achieve these aims. The reasons for this failure are manifold, but the primary reason is that few executives are truly interested in or comprehend the planning process. Most of them are oriented toward problems rather than toward opportunities.

Company size in itself does not make planning easier or less necessary. This point is not universally accepted, however. Some of the managers contacted during the course of this study believe that setting the course is more difficult in small companies and keeping things on course more difficult in large companies. But opinions such as these are probably based more on attitudes than on facts.

For example, long-range planning in a large, diversified corporation with ample planning facilities is not necessarily better or more easily accomplished than in a small, single-product business. The better resources of the larger firm are often offset by conflicts of interest and differences of opinion between unit and headquarters personnel far exceeding those between the key people in a small business.

Conversely, planning is not necessarily more easily accomplished in small companies, because they are more susceptible to rapid changes in market and production cycles than are large firms. In fact, these characteristics lead many small businessmen to regard anything beyond operational planning as superfluous. They rely on their firm's flexibility and short-term responsiveness to be adequate for meeting tomorrow's contingencies and opportunities.

The First Step Toward Improved Planning

Reallocating their time is one of the main accommodations small businessmen must make to improve planning. Planning requires executive time taken from today's problems and operations (which have immediate payout) and applied to the reaching for future benefits (which are always less assured). The shortages of executives to do the planning combined with their relative lack of planning experience make the planning effort in the small company especially difficult.

Although planning in a small business cannot be a Hollywood production, it nevertheless requires as much concern for detail as in larger companies. Detail takes time and specialized skills and when one is in short supply, more of the other must be available. In small firms specialized skills are usually in shortest supply. As a result, executives of small businesses should expect to invest more time than their counterparts in large firms to achieve the same amount and quality of planning output.

Despite the fact that small firms typically must expect to invest more time than large firms *per unit* of planning production, the total amount of time need not be disproportionate. Small firms do not have to plan as widely or as far into the future as large companies.

Executives in small businesses should also recognize that on-the-job experience in a small firm ill prepares a manager to plan. Planning is a specialty as different from other business functions as tennis is from golf and, contrary to common opinion, planning is not an intrinsic part of these and other basic activities. It is a myth that because small company executives wear many hats they necessarily must be good planners.

Planning differs from other functions not only in the form of activities involved but also in the faculties involved; it takes reflective thinking, self-analysis, and the ability to look at the company and its people in ways which at times will be uncomfortable or disquieting. The successful handling of daily operational crises is a poor background for planning.

This point was well illustrated by Wallace Hodes, whose company became part of Corning:

"I always thought working for a big company would be heaven—freedom from pressing money worries, ample production facilities, enough people to handle the work, and so on. But I was simply stunned by the problems of the big business environment when I first encountered them. Big company people talk a different language. The volume of reporting and communicating staggered me. As a small businessman, I had never looked two weeks beyond the present, and now they ask me where I will be in five years and many times in between."

Mr. Hodes further illustrated the difference in the scale of information in big business: "Every four weeks a man comes down from headquarters and tells us how we did versus other companies in the corporation and how we did in terms of the general economy."

Implementing Plans

A further step toward improvement of the planning function occurs when the small company realizes that it must take care in implementing its own plans. Small businesses tend to do a poor job of providing solid connections between planning and execution. Executives of small businesses must recognize that plans will die if they are assumed to have a life-force of their own. Making a plan is only the first step in the attainment of a desired objective. Once committed to a plan, a company must keep it in the forefront of everyone's consciousness. This involves more than establishing reporting procedures and controls; it requires human attention, a quality not always easily engaged and still less easily commanded.

Oddly enough, the very abilities that permit a small business to survive may be the source of the problem. The need to watch costs, to avoid risks the company cannot afford, and to be on top of daily operations may be the factors that prevent the small firm from effectively carrying out the planning process.

Guides for Effective Planning

In establishing planning as a process, the president of the small company should bear in mind that he is launching a process of considerable complexity and delicacy. It is a process of deliberate change that must lead to improvement. Also, it must be value-oriented and must be able to be integrated with other aspects of the business; ultimately it must be effective at the operational level.

Following are some guides for effective planning—things to keep in mind in order to avoid the major pitfalls in deciding the course of future actions.

Effective planning shapes the future. Planning must not be a case of keeping up with the Joneses. Had Henry Ford followed the advice of pundits he would have remained in the bicycle business instead of remaking the map of America. Planning which is mere adaptation to trends, to prognostications about the future, is dangerous mainly because it fails to permit full use of the creative elements within the company.

Effective planning is company-centered; that is, it is based on considerations applying to and arising within this company and not any other. Sound plans are tailored to the specific requirements and capabilities of a particular company and must be based on your company's needs and no other.

Effective planning issues from central ideas. Plans laid in the absence of overall aims or objectives tend to be ill-formed and the results they produce are usually uncertain. The worth of a plan derives as much from management's ideas about the business as from the target of the plan itself.

Effective planning has positive goals. Good plans always aim at creating rather than stopping something; a good plan does not seek to put an end to machine idleness but to raise utilization to levels of profitability. Although negative plans cost more to implement and control than positive plans (because they fail to capture the interest of those whose work is affected), occasionally they may be necessary.

Effective planning is based on careful appraisal. Knowledge of company needs, the probability of reaching a given objective, and the cost of attaining that objective are vital to sound planning. This is not to say that plans should be laid only to achieve those objectives which are certain of attainment and reachable at low cost. To the contrary; some needs are so pressing that there is little choice but to take risks at high cost. But a skilled planner measures the odds for and against a course of action and uses that information and his knowledge of how badly the action is needed before committing the company.

Effective planning calls for specific results. Since plans should be aimed at the attainment of given results, it is only common sense to include in the plans a statement of the results sought in specific terms. Terms of quantity or numerical relationships are especially desirable. Where these are lacking, careful attention must be given to the description of the results sought.

If it proves difficult or impossible to state simply and accurately what the desired results are, take another look at the necessity for the plan. There may be none.

Effective planning has a timetable. Because every business is an economic enterprise, its principal terms are rates, productivity, and other words defining units in time. Thus it is not enough that plans stimulate results; they must also stipulate deadlines. It is also useful to designate checkpoints so that progress in attaining results may be monitored.

Effective planning identifies the executor. The surest way of achieving the results sought by planning is to assign responsibility for results to one man. This is not simple; it forces planners to deal with many questions besides immediate objectives, such as the delegation of authority. There will be times, therefore, when planning will prove impractical even when objectives seem realistic and attainable, because secondary considerations make them uneconomical or organizationally disruptive.

Effective planning lays the basis of control. Although this is a broader and looser requirement than those preceding, it is no less vital. What it means, basically, is to plan only where control can be exercised. Where correction of unacceptable or excessive deviations cannot be made or enforced, planning is a waste of effort. Part of the planning job, therefore, is consideration of the types and extents of controls required for the plan's realization.

3 Organization Structure

It is almost universally held that direct relationships exist between company size and organizational complexity; that is, the variety and numbers of functions and relationships required to provide the company's products or services increase with size. On the other hand, there is nowhere near the same degree of agreement that a similar relationship exists between company size and organizational formality (that is, structural design that establishes and channels relationships and job design that defines responsibilities and authorities).

Executives of small and large companies have fairly sharp differences of opinion about the organizational needs of small businesses. These differences cannot be reconciled easily because there is a dearth of research and information on the subject. Nearly two-thirds of the small company executives surveyed feel strongly that their firms can benefit from being, relatively speaking, structured as formally as larger companies. This belief runs counter to the widely held view that small companies are naturally informal and should stay as informal as possible.

Executives interviewed were quite responsive on the subject of the effects of corporate size on organization. One small company president said: "There comes a time in growth when organization must change. People know what needs to be done and how to do it—but there is so much to do and so little agreement as to who is to do it that everyone is frustrated."

His statement was supported by another executive from a somewhat larger, but still small, company: "There is an enormous difference between a $2 million and a $7 million operation. In going from one to the other we were forced to formalize disproportionately."

Not every person interviewed believed that structural complexity necessarily varies directly with company size. One large company respondent held that small company structures can be rather involved and large company structures quite simple. Of his company he said: "We have a minimum number of people in our power structure, and our management is quite centralized without being an impediment."

Structure and Size

Organization first becomes an economic consideration when a firm becomes too large for one man to run it effectively, and yet is still too small to afford a team of executives with the spectrum of competences required to fully meet the needs of the business. Unfortunately, when this point is reached (by a gradual process), it does not always lead to an organizational shift in the small company. Usually either the top man sees in the situation even greater justification for holding on to his authority, or his inexperience in organization causes him to complicate matters without adding benefits by hiring personnel to do his bidding.

The aim behind a given organizational design is, or should be, the creation of conditions most favorable to the doing of a particular job, to the attainment of particular objectives. The job to be done depends in considerable degree on the size of the company. Hence organization structure should also relate in some fashion to corporate size—a fact that is largely overlooked because the great majority of small businessmen either ignore organization as a differentiating function or design their company's organization after the models of large firms. It is rare to find a small company manager who appreciates both that structure makes a difference in performance and that small companies require organizational arrangements unique to their size.

That organization structures of big companies must differ in major ways from small companies was demonstrated years ago by Graicunas, who showed that 5 people involve 10 channels of communication; 10 people, 45 channels; 100 people, 495 channels; and so on.

Consideration of Graicunas' work leads to the realization that organization configurations suitable to a company when it was one size lose their applicability when the size changes. For example, communications networks appropriate to a 10-man group are inapplicable to a 1,000-man group. This point is confirmed by the fact that high degrees of organizational formality are inimical to change-needs.

Large companies must be organized to offset the natural restrictions of bigness on innovation and adaptability and to foster the capacity to change.

In contrast, organization in the small company should be designed to limit the effects of gratuitous change, subject as it is to more rapidly shifting environmental winds. Small companies—which have advantages in sensitivity and flexibility because of their smaller capital bases and staffs—must be organized to limit responsiveness to relevant environmental fluctuations and to prevent subjective, catastrophic reaction.

These are quite different objectives, and they reveal that large and small companies have different jobs to do.

The Need to Change

The point at which organizational crisis first occurs in a small company varies considerably, depending on the nature of the particular business, the capacities of the key executives, and the managerial attitudes in force. Founder management in one company may become inadequate by the time it employs 25 people, in another not before it has 200. Departmental organization is seldom found in companies with annual sales below $100,000. Companies with annual sales above $1 million but less than $3 million usually have two or three formal-

ized departments; those with sales from $3 million to $6 million, three to five departments; and those with sales from $6 million to $20 million, from five to eight departments.

Production and sales are still most likely to be the first organizational components to appear in small businesses, but marketing and EDP are making their appearance increasingly early in the growth of small firms.

Saul Gellerman believes the problem of maintaining organizational viability occurs most commonly when a business exceeds 1,000 people. He commented: "The problem at that size is that the 'wearing of many hats' no longer assures broadness of scope and flexibility. At 1,000 people and above, it is hard to disseminate information about job needs and opportunities, and so the ability to expand and/or reallocate job responsibilities is equally difficult. As a company gets larger, the typical approach is to try to set up an organizational structure which will keep the company in small units, in effect a series of linked small companies."

Organizations can feel the pinch of size. Peter Scott said: "When a business hits $1 million of pretax profits, it must start to become institutionalized; it also tends that way when there are at least four major functional departments."

Size and Responsibility

When a company reaches the size where one man cannot keep all activities in view, it becomes necessary to reorganize (or, for the first time, organize). By necessity, the first step must be to establish job definitions. Without task differentiation, increasing chaos would be the concomitant of growth. Specialization of work inevitably becomes needed in a growing company to channel the range of individual actions and behavior into predictable and knowable routines.

In small organizations, individual members often have responsibilities that in larger concerns normally are divided among several people. An executive in a small company may handle several unlike functions such as financing, purchasing, and personnel relations. Foremen in smaller shops commonly shoulder responsibilities which are, in larger companies, handled by staff services. In small firms, specialized services are seldom necessary; fewer workers have to be trained and supervised, and relationships generally entail far less formality. Hence administration is simplified, often to the point where overt control and coordination are not needed.

Cost Considerations

Nevertheless, even in small firms avoiding redundancy in decision making is a vital principle of cost control and organization. In most situations, authority should be exercised by a single person, usually the one responsible for executing or accomplishing the task. But in small companies this principle is often recognized more in theory than in practice, with the result that many small companies waste a great deal of time in unnecessary consultation and cross checking before acting.

This waste can be reduced by giving each manager a statement of his responsibilities and authorities written within the embrace of the firm's objectives and policies. This recommendation does not run counter, in fact or spirit, to the sound advice that a small business "stay loose." In fact, it makes possible a high degree of self-guidance, self-discipline, and self-appraisal, all of which favor minimal exercise of direct, restrictive control.

Advisory Committees

Economic considerations in the small company oppose specialization. This raises problems when unusual situations arise that call for special knowledge or contrasting points of view. One answer is for the small company to set up an authoritative, well-constituted group, such as an executive, advisory, or management committee, to provide guidance at the topmost level in matters of the greatest importance to the firm. Such a group can place a wider variety of skills, experience, and sensitivities at the service of a small firm than normally can be found within it.

Although few small companies use such groups, small company executives would be wise to consider their advantages. Small business managers tend to miss the experience that helps them grow into broad-gauged decision makers. A properly constituted group, such as an advisory committee, having at least two noncompany but business-oriented members, offsets that lack.

One small businessman whose company created an advisory committee said that the committee had made the firm take steps it would not otherwise have taken, such as making it clear "who was responsible for what." Recent growth had stretched job responsibilities, created interpersonal tensions, and threatened nonfamily employees. Moving management toward the systematic in this case required delineation of job duties and limits—a requirement which executives of larger companies learn early in their careers. After the responsibilities of each key staff member had been determined, the committee, among other useful functions, served as an appellate body, hearing and resolving jurisdictional disputes that arose as a result of the segregation of responsibilities.*

*See Theodore Cohn, "The Advisory Committee," *The Journal of Accountancy,* October 1965.

4
Controlling

Among the natural advantages of small businesses is that they are in a better position to resist the snowballing of costs that plagues so many large concerns. Ironically, this position does not automatically result in better cost control, probably because the proximity of small business executives to operations creates a false sense of security.

The fact that cost control should be among their paramount concerns is not always recognized by managers in small companies. Many of them feel that their product, marketing, or distribution advantages offer adequate protection from competition.

This is not always the case. The financial vice-president of one small company interviewed described the disaster that nearly occurred when an established cost control program was abandoned: "We nearly went bust in the sixties because somebody decided we couldn't afford the analytically based cost controls we had and that we should get back to the 'practical.' The net result was that when trouble came, we couldn't see it until we were in well over our heads."

Indifference or unwillingness to closely watch and rigorously control costs almost always results in costs that are ruinous or potentially so.

Effective Cost Control

Effective cost control begins when the small business executive consciously seeks to keep his company out of areas in which it probably does not belong—those in which large companies do well. Small business usually comes into or maintains its existence because it provides a specific service to a particular geographical or user market. When it departs from this standard it usually finds itself engaged in a battle for its life. In such battles, cost control, added late and considered a luxury, is an early casualty.

The next step in a cost control program is taken when the small company executive balances his responsibility for spending with finding ways to spend the same amount to create more value, or spending less to create the same value. Although product or procedural stasis is commonly associated with large companies, small companies are more prone to stick longer than they should to the same designs or ways of doing things.

A strong cost accounting system and cost-sensitive controls are essential if the small company expects to stay in business. The ability of the small company executive to put his finger on almost every activity and his experience of running things directly, particularly in the early years of the business, generally result in reluctance to spend money on cost systems.

The most common benefit of increased production volume is lower labor and overhead costs per unit of output, and this fact constitutes the heart of the vulnerability of small companies.

By the very nature of the markets they serve and the

products or services they provide, small companies are usually labor- rather than capital-intensive. In most small companies labor content represents a significant cost area to be especially watched and controlled.

Establishing a Cost Control Program

Following are some steps the small business should consider in setting up a cost control program.

- Use sales forecast figures to make up budgets, showing costs as percentages of those figures and product line contribution to fixed costs and profit.
- Use a perpetual inventory system for high turnover and high value items as a cost control program rather than as an accounting system only.
- Identify patterns of use or purchase patterns on the items that must be stocked to keep the minimum number required to supply customers or to maintain production.
- Give consideration to using the incremental or marginal income concept as an aid in deciding whether to take additional volume at lower than standard prices. The concept is also useful in keeping track of breakeven volume and decisions. The next point is related to this concept.
- Analyze variable costs of sales, broken down by product line, major customer, size, area, or salesmen. A distributor of construction equipment who analyzed variable income contributed by each major product line discovered that he should drop one line because its cost of sales, commission expenses, preparation costs, and warranty adjustments left only 5 percent of sales to pay for fixed costs and contribute to profits while adding no sales advantage.
- Design cost information output so it can be used in other areas of decision making, such as cost data for each process and for machine loading, setting prices of new products on a basis other than following the market, replacing equipment or choosing between lease-or-buy options, and determining economic quantities for major purchases.
- Give close attention to the advisability of accumulating direct costs of labor and material by products. The simple overhead relationship between fixed and variable overhead costs and labor, or between labor and material, should be computed. Unit costs are a useful result. These basic cost data are needed for control (comparing past figures with current and/or planned), price setting, and figuring estimates.
- Be slow to install a standard cost system and then only when its benefits are proved beyond doubt; the installation and maintenance of a standard cost system

require a level of sophistication that is rare in a small business. Moreover, standard costs are most useful where production is expected to be stable long enough to develop truly meaningful, objective standards.
- Give the assignment of cost control responsibility the most careful consideration; successful control in a small company requires a precise definition of who is to control expenditures in each area of the business.

One generalization that applies not only to cost controls but to all management methods is that small companies should be more concerned with the control of the methods chosen rather than with the development of new methods. Picking from available cost controls those that fit the specific company is not easy but can be accomplished better than the routine chore of seeing to it that the method chosen is implemented and used regularly for effective decision making. An informal organizational climate influenced by a few strong managers may permit a variety of controls to be initiated; the same informality will prevent continued effective use of the controls.

Perhaps the last and best advice to be given small business managers is, "Do not spend more on a control system than it will return in savings." A cost control system that is excessive to the important needs of the company is as much a luxury as and potentially more wasteful than an expensive, idle machine.

In designing the cost control program keep in mind the difference between informality and absence of administration and between formality and management. Informality does not indicate that proper direction and control of the business is lacking, nor does formality prove that sound administration exists.

To avoid inappropriate formalism the smaller company should be aware that acquiescence is a poor substitute for independent involvement. Opening up the organization to permit participation is preferable to further specialization and organizational differentiation. Common, baseless fears in small companies can be reduced by such practices as distributing information about company results and permitting or encouraging employees to share in decisions that affect them. More simply, the small business manager should capitalize on the informality and fewer organizational levels which characterize his firm by sharing necessary financial data with responsible employees, opening the doors to the executive suite to include those concerned with change, actively encouraging independent action within a plan framework, and avoiding organizational or specialization moves which are slavish adaptations of big company practices.

5
Recruitment

Not all the handicaps of small business are inherent. Some are self-imposed, and probably nothing illustrates this fact better than an examination of recruitment in small companies. Any firm that wants to survive and prosper needs competent people. Until recently small firms were at some disadvantage in attracting such people. Many business executives therefore fell into the habit of thinking poorly of the abilities of small companies to attract able people. The following statements expressed by two field respondents are typical.

"Big business gets better people because it offers the competent man stability and more room to grow."

"Small business has weaker recruiting abilities and must take the personnel leavings from big business. It is very hard for small business to attract experienced men from big business."

Even in those who hold more moderate views, the suspicion persists that small firms have recruitment disadvantages, as other statements indicate.

"In finding people, small business is at a disadvantage at the $2 million sales range because good management candidates have questions about survival and growth. At $5 million to $10 million, a small business will find it easier to attract people because the potential new employee sees room to move. Only when they are over $20 million are small firms generally on a par with large companies in terms of recruitment."

"In the matter of attracting personnel, small com-panies probably do as well as big firms in all but the top jobs. I suspect that the competition for top talent favors the large companies because most people think they offer greater opportunities and more career leverage. I don't think this is true, but most people do."

"A big company will generally pay one salary grade higher than a small one. This is one reason small business has a problem getting good people. Worse, salary differentials are harder to justify in a small business. Most people seem to find out what others are earning, and if the explanations are not very solid, the effect on morale can be serious."

Although many of the problems in small firms are thought to be caused by a genuine inability to attract or afford top talent, it is far more likely that they stem from other sources, such as the traditional adherence by small business managers to the view that manpower is to be bought as cheaply as possible and that it is entirely an expense and not an asset. Such a view is neither necessary nor economically justified, and it causes small firms to underrate their manpower needs and capacities for attracting better people. This view becomes pernicious when it is expressed in the tendency to regard gifted executives as luxuries the small firm cannot afford.

The gaps between available skills and skills actually used constitute a measure of the condition and fortunes of a company. Many small companies underemploy; that is, they employ lesser skills than are available to them internally or in the marketplace. Even where these gaps are currently small, the rising levels of industrialization and technology tend to increase them. Hence the improvement of recruitment should be of particular interest to the small company that intends to become or remain successful.

Hiring the Right People

Regardless of the assumption about the advantages of large company employment, there is convincing evidence that small firms can improve their competitive position by giving proper attention to hiring the right personnel. In the face of growing corporate giantism, the small company is becoming increasingly attractive to competent men and women, many of whom fear being robotized in the large corporation.

The recruiter for the small business should exploit the advantages that a small company can offer high-potential personnel. His basic approach should go something like this: "A small business, because it is small, has many advantages lacking in a large firm. It can employ people with broad skills; offer greater challenges and a wider variety of experiences; offer more authority and earlier opportunities to make significant contributions; give more immediate satisfactions; and yield earlier rewards than a large firm can." All these factors have a definite and increasing recruitment value for the small firm.

Opportunities Offered by Small Firms

Typical of the opportunities small businesses can offer high-potential people are the following.

1. *A better chance of becoming top man.* In a small company the odds in favor of a man becoming the top executive are far better than in a large company even if the pattern of succession cannot be seen at present.

2. *Personal contacts are far richer.* The close relation between employees and management and the greater intimacy with customers and markets in a small business are factors in its favor. A small firm gives its managers opportunities to be where the action is: for example, relations with the top brass are more likely to be face to face than indirect. In contrast, the man in a large organization usually sees only a small part of the total picture. He finds it more difficult to alter the scheme of things and to extract information from, or force it through, formal channels of communication.

3. *Quicker assumption of power.* Competent men want authority and want it fast. Men in larger companies learn to become more satisfied with their salaries than with the scope or level of their responsibilities. The economics of small businesses facilitates the early assumption of significant authority.

4. *Accelerated experience.* Moderate-size companies cannot afford large-scale training programs; they develop executives primarily by example and on-the-job experience. Furthermore, the scope of work each executive performs is usually more varied than that of a comparable person in a large company.

5. *Easier human relations.* Smaller companies are more informal than larger ones, an attraction to many people. The informality goes beyond the absence of rigid organization and procedures; it extends to dress, flexibility of working hours, and a general atmosphere of greater ease. The human side of small companies can be warmer and more fun than that of big companies.

6. *Recognition and rewards for good performance come more quickly.* A small business offers faster performance feedback and better awareness of one's value and contribution. It is not handicapped by complicated compensation policies, appraisal systems, or rigid reporting structures. Moreover, the small business can better tailor rewards to its employees' needs. For example, the man who wants a few extra days of vacation for personal reasons or a summer job for one of his children can be more easily accommodated in a small firm than in a large one.

7. *Job security is at least as good as in big companies.* There has been growing recognition that the successful small company offers employment security at least equal to that of its larger corporate competitors. The reduction in large business employment caused by the decline in economic activity in 1970–1971 was disproportionately higher and more widely reported than that in smaller businesses. The small business tends to be more cost-conscious and less prone to overstaff (visibility alone makes that hard to do).

8. *Demands on personal and family life are minimized.* A small company gives a man a better chance to establish community roots. He can raise his family without repeatedly moving and going through the discomforts of selling and buying a house, requiring his children to change schools frequently, and working for social acceptance in a new, strange community.

To recruit successfully and at costs in keeping with its size, the small company must observe several precautions. It should develop clear-cut recruiting and hiring policies. In doing so it will need to recognize and, where possible, to reconcile standards, biases, and myths that vitally affect recruitment. One example is the almost universal tendency to search for new personnel on the basis of tenure; executives of small companies prefer employees who will remain with the firm for a long period of time. This prejudice should be junked; people should be hired because they are truly needed and can produce the results desired, not because they can be expected to stay forever. Tenure, in and by itself, has little value.

One small business hired a 58-year-old controller who had been unacceptable to large companies because of his age. He worked for the small company for 6 years, contributed his 35 years of experience to its problems, and left its financial affairs and systems in solid shape for his successor whom he had trained.

Another point to keep in mind is that if the businessman does not really intend to delegate specific responsibility almost immediately, he should not promise to do so. If he understands this, and is really willing to delegate, employment in his company can be almost irresistible to the high-potential man or woman.

6
Directing: The Human Factor

One of the most commonly held ideas in industry is that attracting, using, and retaining competent manpower are among the most difficult problems facing any company. Field respondents felt, generally speaking, that differences between small and large companies are especially great in the area of personnel relations.

Small companies suffer the consequences of personnel problems more than large firms, partly because managers in small companies tend to underestimate and underutilize the available human resources. Hence one of the principal ways for small companies to materially improve their performance is by raising the contributions of all personnel to the limits of their potential.

Sources of Problems in the Small Company

Personnel problems in small businesses are distinctive in a number of ways.

1. Small firms, although they have much narrower ranges of competence from which to draw, must nevertheless deal with most of the functions that are dealt with in large organizations; however, the smaller volume of transactions is not accompanied by proportionate shrinkages in the range or depth of needed capabilities.

2. Small firms have less experience in and time for recruiting capable people and developing them properly; they invest much less of their monetary and intellectual resources than large companies in acquiring, identifying, and developing people with outstanding skills.

3. Small firms have comparatively little key-man mobility; executive turnover is lower and average job tenure longer than in large companies (without obvious, offsetting benefits).

4. Small firms can be dominated by extraordinary people more easily than large firms; by the very nature of their origins or need for survival, most small companies have at least one such person.

The first personnel problem discussed above causes special problems in small companies because it is rare to have even one man for each major function. The typical small business cannot afford manager specialists and, therefore, demands of its key people a wider range of involvement than do large companies (which can scarcely function without specialists). Executives of small businesses must, therefore, comprehend something of the techniques that apply to a wide range of business activities, such as production, finance, planning, controlling, sales management, sales promotion, training, and motivation. For the safety of their firms, these executives must also acquire some skill in evaluating economic conditions and in dealing with minority stockholders, employees, customers, and the public in general. One result of dealing with so many matters is that executives of small businesses have little time to develop a deep knowledge of any particular area.

In this lack lies one of the great dangers to small firms. The small business that fails to recognize the danger of its weakness in knowledge and to seek to overcome that lack by the best means available is drifting with the tide. The poor quality of plant layout, production methods, financial controls, and marketing practices in so many small companies testifies to their failure to recognize and fill gaps in managerial expertise.

The application of goal setting, regular performance reviews, and compensation methods tied to productive results—all established techniques—has a quick payoff in small firm managerial development. Because of the relatively lower executive turnover of smaller firms, there is a greater need for upgrading personnel, one procedure that is feasible in an organization where retention of personnel is considered a goal in itself.

Interpersonal Skills

A subject of great interest to persons interviewed in the study was the difference between small and large firms in their dependence on interpersonal skills. A frequently voiced opinion was that executives of large businesses must have high people skill but that managers in small businesses need not. One manager holding that opinion cited the fact that "management in a larger company is essentially the administration of other people."

Questionnaire results reinforced these views. Many executives believe that management of a small business can be highly individualistic but that management of a large one cannot. This is probably true, in the sense that the closer working relationships in the small company permit greater self-expression and less conscious attention to the problems of getting along with one's colleagues, coordinating, and communicating. But it is patently false in the sense that the small company's lesser dependence on interpersonal skills permits its personnel to act in disregard of the needs of their fellow workers.

It is largely a matter of balance, no matter what the size of the firm. Any firm that wishes to operate successfully must permit the expression of individual interests and skills while simultaneously keeping the firm on course. And in this regard small firms have the advantage. Idiosyncratic behavior can usually be more comfortably and productively dealt with in a small company than it can be in a large one. Here are comments from several study respondents who thought along these lines.

"One does not have to be a good manager of people in small business. The satisfactions are more closely related to the work than in large companies. Small companies can more readily adapt to individual personalities."

"The main aptitudes a man needs in a large company are selling ability and skill with people. Small businessmen need a wider variety of skills and, therefore, are not likely to be so adept in human relations."

"The interpersonal skill is the most important ability of an executive in big business. If he cannot get along with his subordinates, peers, and supervisors, he is without influence and impotent as a manager."

"One reason MBA's fall on their faces in large companies is that they have a lot of knowledge of management science but too little about how to get along with people."

Two other statements brought into focus more unusual aspects of the question.

"People can be dealt with more directly in small companies. Big firms have to use more deception in dealing with their people."

"Sure, there are small business executives who are totally indifferent to people. I don't know how they get away with it, but it is undeniable that many small companies are run by men who have practically no feeling for human relationships. This is probably a function of two things: first, many people who are rejected by the large corporations have to work somewhere; second, some people in this world are attracted by rough, gruff people."

In an article relating to this subject Eli Ginzberg wrote: "Large organizations teach people who work for them to play it cool in order to get along. This is the main road to conformity. A large organization is a political organization. One is not supposed to get into trouble if he hopes to go anywhere. He does not get good marks for getting into difficulty. Consequently, everybody quickly learns how the game is played. They learn to keep their mouths shut."*

There were, of course, some dissenting opinions. D. W. Vaughn, president of Southern Indiana Electric & Gas Company, thinks interpersonal skill is more needed in small firms than is generally thought: "Only a mighty small company can operate successfully with top people lacking people orientation. People aren't as subservient as they used to be; they have much more self-respect."

The Ohio utilities executive previously quoted said: "It may have been true that people orientation may not have been important in small companies in the past, but the increased mobility of employees and increased employee opportunities surely must tend to wipe out differences in this respect between small and large companies."

*Eli Ginzberg, "The Impact of Changing Attitudes Toward Work," *Journal of College Placement*, April–May 1969.

Two other comments were more strongly stated. Mr. Carothers, executive vice-president of Union Electric Company, said: "People being people, they are deterrents to corporate effectiveness as often as not. Therefore, skill in dealing with people is essential in the small business."

The executive in the large capital goods company said: "A man can work up to a high position in a large company and remain a small boy. He can't do that in a small company; that is, he can't move up without being effective in interpersonal relationships."

The difference in leadership styles necessary to businesses of different sizes was expressed by Mr. Marantz, who felt that a dictatorial style is capable of being used (though not necessarily desirable) in an organization employing up to 1,000 people. He noted that when the firm has fewer than 1,000 people the top man can make the major decisions, probably with the help of some other people. Running a company that employs more than 1,000 people becomes a group task even though carrying out decisions remains an individual responsibility.

The capital goods company executive called attention to the danger of overstressing the importance of interpersonal competence: "The idea that managers should have interpersonal competence can be a handicap when it leads to oversimplification. In my experience, one seldom finds other forms of brilliance in the executive who has good skills with people."

To illustrate the danger of repressing individuality, the manager of a large company related an anecdote of how a proposed acquisition had not been consummated. In spite of a long investigation, which fully confirmed the view of everyone involved that the acquisition was desirable, no one person would take the responsibility of making the decision, and the proposal never got off the ground.

Thus it would appear that small firms have the advantage over large ones in being less dependent on behavioral conformity. Franklin A. Moss, vice-president, finance, J. I. Kislak, Inc., summed it up this way: "Small companies can stand the individual and his idiosyncrasies better than the big company."

Wallace Hodes commented: "Oddballs can't live in the big business environment. Big business requires conformity; that is, men not only have to do things in the same or similar ways, but they also have to create acceptance of themselves as fulfillers of norms. There is no place in the big company for the fellow without regard for time, standards, or folkways. The big company environment inevitably depersonalizes employees.

"The big companies hand out year pins in an effort to offset this tendency and to heal the breaches of factionalism, but it doesn't help. An executive from the parent company passes out the pins to men he hardly knows—so efficiently and rapidly that the men have no chance for personal contact with him.

"Wives are left home. In the old days whenever we had a bash, the wives would be present and would get all fired up to the point where they, too, felt that 'this is our company' and would send their men out in the mornings with a 'Go to it, tiger.' Now the wives know little more than the company takes their men away from them for a night."

7
Stockholder Agreement

The number of shareholders is often proportionate to size. With few exceptions, large firms have many shareholders, and the shares are traded in a public securities market. Although the shares of small companies may be publicly held, more commonly they are narrowly held and there is no market for them, public or otherwise. This lack of marketability and the concentration of ownership in one person, or a few at most, are the basis for much of the psychic energy waste and problems of small business managers.

A current stockholders' agreement is needed for almost all small companies—a contractual understanding for which the owner of a publicly held security has no need because of the availability of a market for and the value it places on his shares.

The small business manager-stockholder usually has the bulk of his personal fortune invested in the shares of his company. Security for his family in case of death, disability, or retirement is moot unless he has provided during his lifetime for the value and disposition of his shares. Without a market in which to sell his stock and set a value on it, the shareholder in the small company often makes management decisions which are aimed not at the best objective interests of the company but at doing what he thinks is best for his family and estate.

A properly drawn agreement can go far toward solving the problem. It should include the setting of a value for the shares, preferably by annual agreement or by formula; terms of payment in case of death, disability, retirement, or disagreement (considering the financial needs of the company and the individuals); limitations on who can buy or receive the shares (to prevent undesirables from becoming part of a group which often acts more like a partnership than a true corporation); provision for insurance, if relevant (to minimize cash requirements on redemption of shares on death); provision for salaries, expenses, vacations, duties (to avoid unpleasant arguments); options as to who must offer and who can or must buy and when (generally, death and disability require the shares to be offered and the corporation to buy); and arbitration procedures.*

Our purpose is not to design a stockholder agreement, but to point out that the relations between a small group of manager-stockholders and the resolution of the inevitable changes that time alone brings are substantively different in the small company by virtue of the size factor, and that the concern and energies of small business managers can be dissipated in dissension and even end in corporate dissolution in the absence of an agreement that is hammered out between the shareholders *before* the problems arise.

*See Martin J. Milston and Theodore Cohn, "Business and Personal Aspects of Stockholder Agreements," *The Journal of Accountancy,* October 1967.

8
Using Information Effectively

Information and communications were two areas of great interest to the executives interviewed in the field. Most of them believe that communications differ widely between large and small companies.

There is less face-to-face contact in large companies and a greater need, therefore, to devote more time to generating, transmitting, using, and storing information.

The growing complexity of business and the increasing use of information-producing devices by competing firms strongly suggest that the small businessman can no longer safely run his business by the seat of his pants, however good his intuitions are. Small businesses face a growing need to operate on a basis of knowledge; they must have better information on hand and use it more effectively than they have in the past.

How Information Serves Small Firms

This point is supported by looking at the most important reasons small businesses fail—deficient planning, overinvestment, unrealistic pricing, inadequate sales, and failure to control costs. Each of these reasons can be attributed to lack of managerial know-how, but each, in its own way, can also be blamed on the failure to muster the information and knowledge needed for successful pursuit of organizational goals. Not even the features of

flexibility and fast response time can help the small business that is operating blindly.

The notion that small businessmen are fast on their feet has justification only when they operate on the basis of information. When they work primarily on opinion, flexibility tends to deteriorate into indecisiveness, and energy into waywardness.

Although information is as vital to small businessmen as to large, many executives of small businesses believe that a sense of, a feel or a smell of, how the business is doing is as good as having specific information. As a result, small businesses usually suffer from a chronic lack of information on which to act.

Small businessmen are most deficient in their knowledge of the determining factors outside their companies—customers' needs and changing social, distribution, and environmental patterns. They are usually on more solid ground in areas of internal knowledge—payroll costs, product pricing, current backlog. The head of a $5 million manufacturing firm was able to reel off the weekly salaries of most of his employees and how much overtime premium had cost the previous week. But, he was ignorant of prices charged by competitors, whether his share of the market was changing (in fact, what his share was), how his customers used his product, and what the changing attitudes and laws on pollution might mean to his business several years in the future.

Financial Information Systems

Lack of financial analysis is a problem common to most small businesses. Although many executives of small businesses regard even a quarterly income statement and balance sheet as unnecessary, these vital documents should be prepared monthly in sufficient detail to pinpoint each revenue and cost area and the financial position of the company. Marginal income contribution for each product or product line, as well as the operating results for the entire operation, should be presented. Whenever possible, statements should be prepared for the current year to date, and against a forecast or budget.

Comparisons, trends, and ratios are keys to using financial statements. The ratio of net income to net worth (return on investment) should be measured against the company's own plan and industry statistics.

Small business should also learn to make use of calculative techniques commonly employed in large firms, such as capital budgeting, discounted cash flow, return on investment, and return on assets managed. It may happen that sound business strategy in a small firm will call for action contrary to that indicated by the results of the techniques. For example, they may show the company's leasing of a computer to be economically marginal at best, but that a computer may be needed nonetheless to attract the kinds of employees it otherwise could not hire. Techniques that illustrate the relative values of alternative decisions are available to small companies, rarely used as they are.

That judgment is a key ingredient in all decisions in which objective data must also be used has further meaning in the small business. Organized data and financial controls act as a brake on the individually created plan or scheme that might, without such analysis or tests of reasonableness, send the company down a hazardous route.

In many small businesses only a few items of information are critical to the control of operations, and finding them should be a prime concern. Finding these key items takes ingenuity and a clear understanding of what the business does. The significant kinds of information needed by small firms usually relate to their sensitive areas, the factors which are functions of how operations are going, the values they add.

For example, one study respondent described how his company, a steel and aluminum fabricator ($6 million to $7 million in volume) found that labor cost per ton of steel or pound of aluminum shipped in each of three departments was the best single indicator of how the company was doing. It not only showed what the efficiency of the factory was; the figures were also invaluable in estimating jobs. For the relatively unsophisticated management of this company, labor cost per ton was broadly understood and used throughout the organization.

The Importance of Pricing

Small business executives interested in becoming better informed about their firm's affairs should keep in mind that approximately half of all the failures in small businesses can be traced to a product or service that was being sold at the wrong price. This can be regarded as a failure to know costs, since an accurate knowledge of costs must be the first step in setting prices.

Small companies that base pricing policy solely on costs and not on the values as seen by the customers lose profits. Firms in a changing-style industry or that provide a unique service can set more profitable pricing policies by being sensitive to the short-lived novelty of their products and the value of their service to the customer.

A small business can afford much less than a large business to service customers who will not pay an adequate price and maintain a product line it is forced to sell at a loss. The small business must know, therefore, a good deal about its cost of sales and selling and distribution costs.

9
Innovation

The fate of every company is determined by how well it meets the necessity of doing something better than its competitors. Maintaining the capacity to be superior in some respect calls for deliberately changing what a company does, and involves expending some portion of a company's resources—time and talent as well as money. Small companies are no exception to these survival requirements, although few of them exhibit awareness of how to fulfill them.

Small Companies Need to Innovate

H. Alan Stein, vice-president, marketing, Shiman Manufacturing Company, stated the case for the psychological requirements for renewal and innovation in small companies: "Unless you see the necessity for change, things don't change and they become dull. Man wants change and interest. This is as true for a small as for a big business."

Large companies, with their many specialists, can carry on a continual improvement program (and are almost forced to in order to remain viable). Small companies, on the other hand, do not have this imperative and often fail to engage in any form of improvement activity because their key men and resources are engrossed in immediate concerns, the "now" problems of the firm. This preoccupation can prove fatal to a firm when it precludes work being done to keep the company abreast of the market, organizationally lean, and operationally effective. The work of anticipating and meeting the need for change (innovation) should receive special attention in small companies, for the simple reason that they, in comparison with large companies, place excessive reliance on being effective in the here and now.

There are no limitations on innovation inherent in being small. In some small firms, for example, a considerable volume of product-related research is carried on by highly qualified scientific and technical personnel. The evidence available points to the fact that innovation—in whatever area it takes place—is unpredictable with respect to size of firm and resources utilized. Many important developments have come from the work of a small number of people working with limited resources. The capabilities of people are more important to the birth of ideas than any material resource.

Blocks to Innovation

The principal stumbling blocks to making progressive change on a systematic basis in small companies are listed here.

● The typical small company has few uncommitted resources; literally everything is being used to the full. There is little reserve left in staff, procedures, or equipment. Running the enterprise takes all the company's available energies, leaving practically nothing for self-improvement.

• Most managers in small companies tend to reject the thought of expense for things that can't be seen, measured, or resold, and to regard themselves more the employers of money and merchandise than of people.

• Small companies that do innovate (as exemplified by "brain companies" headed by inventors or scientists who became entrepreneurs) often do not go beyond exploiting the competence of their founders or one extraordinary individual. These abilities are soon exploited and often become barriers to the introduction of new ideas.

Each of these blocks to innovation must be removed if the small company is to become and/or remain prosperous. Managers in small businesses who are determined to achieve improved results through innovation must ask themselves: "How much innovation is enough?" This question demands careful answers; small business can die as easily from too much or misdirected creative work as from none. More small businesses go broke from overambition than from inertia.

Guidelines

A successful program of innovation in a small company begins with establishing guidelines for creative efforts. Since the guidelines cannot be too precise, a list of them is likely to contain a mixture of propositions that are generally true for all kinds and sizes of companies along with those that apply specifically to the company involved. The following list, compiled from the authors' experiences, exemplifies this point.

• Every commercial enterprise, whatever its size, exists for the purpose of spending money to create value in excess of the money spent.

• A small company makes its living by filling needs the big company cannot afford to fill (by producing products or services in response to variables inimical to large-scale production, such as short delivery time or custom features).

• The small company does best in a market that is stable for its products (a small business that must continually move into new markets has picked wrong products).

• The small company is favored by products that have short production runs; the longer its production runs, the more vulnerable to competition from larger companies a small company is.

• Great variability of demand, seasonally or volumetrically, favors small company operations.

• Small companies should look for products that

are required in high quality; high-volume methods which favor large companies are often deficient in the quality of the article or service produced.

• Increasing product variation and complexity create new opportunities that favor exploitation by small companies.

• Companies that serve markets highly sensitive to product features must take pains to avoid getting trapped into product stasis. (Market *stability* at times results from design *mobility*.)

• Small companies should strive for recognized degrees of exclusivity for their products or services; because the investment capacity of small companies limits their investments in production facilities and expertise, they benefit less from freezing product designs than large companies.

• Small firms are favored when their products or services cannot easily be combined with other products or services, either in production or sales.

• Small companies should resist having a full product line when it diminishes having a distinctive line; the small company competes most effectively when its items appeal to customers because they are distinctive rather than because of gradations among them.

• Small companies that risk large portions of their resources in projects which do not offer the possibility of learning early whether the innovations will be successful engage in unjustifiable and, possibly, deadly risks. (Seven out of eight hours of time devoted to product development in this country are spent on projects that do not achieve commercial success.)

• Small companies should avoid products that require long investment of time; risks rise in direct proportion to the stretching of time between the first investment and the earliest possibility of payoff.

• Opportunities for small business relate to the stage of maturity of the industry or product involved. Small businesses tend to be important producers or suppliers of components, of products in early stages of development, while large firms tend to dominate the markets for older, established products.

One technically oriented small company president said he saw his company as a revolving door of new ideas. The source of the ideas was limitless, although many came from castoffs of big companies. More important, he felt the place of his company was to develop the ideas to the point of commercial feasibility, when large companies acquired them for production and marketing, both of which required capital resources beyond the capacity of the small company.

Whether his company has taken the trouble to provide such market and innovation guidelines or not, every small company executive must recognize that the part of the innovation cycle his company must do best is accurate assessment of the financial and other risks involved in implementing ideas. It must do this with tough-minded objectivity because of the high mortality of new ideas and the fact that any single change in a small company has a much greater effect, proportionately, than in a large company.

The strongest reason for innovation is that deliberate change is the basic requirement of business survival. And when change is made to order, corporate life becomes more exciting and rewarding. Thus innovative firms tend to attract and hold innovative men and to bring the entrepreneurs hidden in the corporate woodwork out in the open. This, perhaps, is the most important benefit of all.

10
The Entrepreneurial Factor

A mixed benefit to all firms is the entrepreneur—the creative business mentality. Although such a person cannot be accommodated easily in any environment, small firms are in the best position to benefit from his employment.

This point was touched on by a respondent who has had a notable career in several very large companies and who now acts as a member of boards of directors and a consultant: "Big business tends to smother the entrepreneur. In large firms entrepreneurs usually are at the top; further down they get smothered. That's why enterprising fellows running their own shows can often beat the pants off big companies in the smaller segments of their business."

A different approach was expressed by a respondent who had worked for both small and large companies. He said that top management in small companies was usually the source of initiative. In large companies this was rarely so because the function of top management was more concerned with approval of new ideas than creating them. Keeping a company on a predetermined course is easier in the large companies if the initiating and approving functions are separate; it may also make the course narrower.

Sherman Fairchild is probably a classic example of the entrepreneurial breed. He said: "The truth is that the man who just thinks of making money usually doesn't make much money. You've got to have your eye not on the money but on the job."*

Jeno Paulucci, who built Chun King into a large business, said: "An entrepreneur can do things no big company can. He can say, 'I want to be in a position where I can put an idea into effect. I don't want to have to sell it to four or five different levels of people. If my idea loses, *I* lose; if it wins, *I* win.' You can't do that in many big corporations."

For a while, William Lear headed a good-size public company, Lear, Inc. But he quit in frustration when his board of directors refused to let him build his now-famed Lear jet. "Why, I might as well have been the janitor there," he said. "At least the janitor could decide on his own where he wanted to sweep."

Qualities of the Entrepreneur

What qualities do entrepreneurs need? "They must have vision," says Sherman Fairchild, "as contrasted with just having a dream. We have lots of dreamers, but not many entrepreneurs. The dreamer figures, 'Wouldn't it be nice to have so-and-so?' but he doesn't have any idea

*This and succeeding quotations on entrepreneurs named in this section of the briefing are taken from an article in *Forbes* entitled "The Incurables," July 1, 1969, pp. 21–60.

how he is going to accomplish it. Real talent has organized vision. The fellow who says, 'Wouldn't it be nice to have an automobile that ran on half the amount of gas? Think of all the money it could make,' is a dreamer. I say to him, 'Come up with an idea on how you are going to accomplish this.' "

Bill Lear says, "I'm not a good manager. I have an enormous distaste for management. Every minute I spend on it makes me just that much less useful at what I am good at; what I am good at is interphasing. That's not the same as being an inventor. An inventor thinks of things that have never been done before. An interphaser is a guy who puts together things that already exist and makes new and better combinations of them." Lear regards his Lear jet as an example of interphasing. "I wanted to make it so bad I could taste it," he says, explaining why he quit the company.

Jeno Paulucci says much the same thing in different words: "It's not just a question of long hours and hard work. It's guts. You have to go at it with sheer determination. Otherwise the pitfalls will put you off. This is why big companies have to go out and acquire smaller ones. There is a quality in starting a business that only an entrepreneur can provide. My accolades to Reynolds for what they've done since they took over Chun King. But no big company can do as good a job as the individual entrepreneur."

Significantly, one trait all these successful entrepreneurs share is a belief in the importance of supplementing their own talents with those of others. They know their limitations.

"The most important thing in business," says Nelson Harris, another business builder, "is to have people work with you, not for you." Even Lear, who has a reputation for being a lone wolf, emphasizes people: "The greatest mistake I ever made was hiring the second-best man for the job. You pay a terrible penalty for that."

Sherman Fairchild waxes eloquent on the subject of getting the best people. As an entrepreneur he gets as much satisfaction out of finding and keeping top-notch people as he does out of devising new organizational tools or inventing devices such as the aerial camera. He said: "One thing I try to do is regard my executives as partners. My father used to tell me, 'Son, don't worry about how much money you're going to make. Get the right guy in and make him a lot of money and that's all you'll need.' I've always followed that advice."

Fairchild has thought a good deal about the characteristics he wants in his executives: "I look for the ability to study a situation and not be blinded by a lot of past statistics that say it can't be done. Sure it's going to be tough. If it wasn't, some dope would have done it

already. The man I want thinks the thing through. He thinks, 'What are the factors that must be put together?' You can't decide this on an accountant's report. There are too many factors that just don't show up in the figures. What I want is to surround myself with entrepreneurs. A foreman in a shop can be an entrepreneur if he takes existing things and puts them together in a new way. That guy usually ends up being head of the company."

Small Businesses and Entrepreneurs

This mixture of entrepreneurial views clarifies at least two important characteristics about the relationship between small businesses and entrepreneurs. First, small firms are the best vehicle for the entrepreneur, but they must organize as much to contain the risks as to exploit the advantages of having such a person. Second, the entrepreneur is usually more concerned with self-expression than with organization building. To him an enterprise is little more than a vehicle for the attainment of his personal goals. He is rarely inclined to see it as an entity that produces goods and results and is, therefore, deserving of continuance after he has achieved his own objectives.

One respondent noted that a typical complaint of the small businessman whose firm has grown to the point where he can no longer do everything himself is, "When I ran everything, I used to love my work. Now that I can't, I don't any more." Small businesses are developed by entrepreneurs who are creative and spend long hours building their companies. They usually have such talent in marketing, engineering, or accounting that it overcomes their weaknesses.

The realization that the job has changed from one of immediate task satisfaction to people management and indirect controls affects small businessmen in different ways.

In the opinion of a large company executive, "The executive in a larger company becomes more remote, not because he wants to but because of the needs of the organization. Activities such as planning, research and development, personnel, industrial relations, and financial matters all take a sizable portion of his available time."

One respondent manager said: "In big business, the chief executive will set the tone even more than will the type of industry. For example, if a big business is run by an accounting man, he will determine policies primarily with an accounting approach even if it is a consumer-oriented company."

D. A. Eberly agreed: "Regardless of company size,

the chief executive sets the style of management (1) by setting standards, (2) by his personal qualifications, and (3) by his own values."

Dr. Andorka said: "The strong ego which is an incalculable aid in building a business unfortunately is also the basic reason so many small businesses never make it into the big leagues. In contrast to the pontificating of so many managers, the groans and agonies of a small business are never heard. If it could, it would say, 'I (the company) have outgrown my management.'"

H. Alan Stein agreed: "The small businessman is the individualist who puts *things* first—the guy who is tough for a large company to swallow."

William L. West went even further: "As a company grows in size the pioneers who founded it almost inevitably lose control of the firms they started."

11

The Chief Executive and Delegation

Speaking of the chief executive officers in small companies, Tinham Veale II, chairman and president of Alco Standard Corporation, was quoted as saying: "Small companies are the backbone of this country, but all too often owners–managers of small companies hit a plateau when sales reach the $5 million mark. At that point they can't seem to expand further. The company's head finds himself devoting too much time to legal, accounting, administrative, and financial problems that he simply is not equipped to handle, and neglecting the production and engineering problems which he is an expert in solving."*

Mr. Veale explained that the owners of more than 50 relatively small, progressive specialty concerns had accepted his invitation to be "relieved of bureaucracy" and to become "profit centers" of Alco.

Merging into a larger company which has the full range of managerial and technical skills is an attractive and often lifesaving step for the small company that has reached the limit of its own management development. It requires a dramatic and conscious step for the entrepreneur to give up pushing the buttons and making the decisions and become a manager. If he cannot take the step, a merger may be the best solution.

*Robert E. Bedingfield, "A Specialist in Putting Pieces Together," *The New York Times,* June 8, 1969.

Presidents of small companies feel pinched for time for firsthand contacts and observation (personnel, sales, and marketing) while large company presidents are aware of insufficient time to devote to the rational business activities (planning, thinking, reading).

Applying Managerial Techniques

There are, however, some notable differences in the application of management techniques. In the larger organization, the chief executive gives control and direction by functioning as a mediator, compromiser, negotiator, and court of last resort so that the various programs, promotions (ideas or products), conflicts, and other problems generated by the size of the organization can be resolved. Sometimes, respondents admitted that the solutions are tainted by personal influence, are politically contrived, or are subject to vested interests.

Conversely, a good deal of the activity described as management action is no more than the force of the system that the company is heir to. "This is the way it is going to be, because we have always done it this way" is the way this fact is expressed, disguised and subtle though the reasoning appears.

Leo Siebert, general manager, Mundt Perforated Metals Corporation, pointed out: "One common mistake small businessmen make is that when they delegate they think they have totally renounced responsibility. They cannot give a man responsibility without defining his job, the performance expected of him, the controls and limits on him, and at the same time continue, of course, to support the man."

Effective delegation is essential to Mr. Siebert's concept. The small businessman who cannot delegate will remain a small businessman if he stays alive at all. To grow or even to survive, any business must have skills in all main functions—production, marketing, administration, and finance. These skills can be exercised only by people with authority in their own right. Because of the overwhelming truth of this statement, questions on delegation were specifically addressed to field respondents.

In Mr. Baum's opinion, "A business becomes big, meaning that the president must delegate, when there are 500 or more employees. Then, one of the major problems becomes getting to the top man. People cannot get answers. The result is that change takes place slowly."

Frank Moss observed: "One responsibility of the chief executive is to create an environment for employees that encourages and activates the 'will do' from the potential of the 'can do.' The chief executive must create this atmosphere even though he is concerned with acquisitions, financial needs, technical progress, manpower development, and joint ventures. Management has responsibility to an employee to help discover the areas where he may require assistance, to build the job around his competence, not to force him to fit into a preconceived notion of what a particular position should be. In any company, large or small, the basis of survival greatly depends on fellow executives."

Leon A. Marantz observed: "At certain levels in big business the chief executive cannot impress; he must delegate. The profit center policy required or used by big business tends to keep managers away from each other. Therefore, it is not as useful as others make it out to be."

Even when the top executive decides to share his work, he does not always do so effectively. He may insist in subtle or obvious ways that his subordinates adopt his suggestions, his way of doing things, his instructions. When the company reaches the point where one-man management is no longer possible, and that man refuses to delegate some significant portion of his work, the overall quality of administration soon declines. Following that, the company falters and usually falls back.

Conclusion

Our aim in this Briefing has been to describe the management differences between small and big companies and recommend the directions small company managers should take to improve the conduct of their firms. Although large companies are gradually increasing their share of the American economy, there will probably remain substantial products and services which will be best handled through smaller organizations.

To survive in a big company environment, to balance profitability within risk limits, and to manage the business so that it attracts and keeps competent people who can provide creative responses to change and be the source of continuity—these are proper areas of concern for which the small business executive must realize there are special problems and solutions unique to the size of his company.

Appendix
Basis of the Survey

Table 1. Are functions of management more difficult in small than in large businesses?

	More Difficult in Small Businesses	Percent	More Difficult in Large Businesses	Percent	Uncertain or No Answer	Percent	Total Responses	Percent
Small company presidents	46	43	58	55	2	2	106	100
Large company presidents	13	14	76	84	2	2	91	100
Total	59	30	134	68	4	2	197	100

Table 2. Functions seen by presidents of small companies as more difficult in smaller companies.

Function	Number of Mentions	Percent of Total Answers
Planning	37	38
Organizing	21	22
Controlling	16	16
Communicating	12	12
Directing	12	12
Total	98	100

Table 3. Functions seen by presidents of large companies as more difficult in large companies.

Function	Number of Mentions	Percent of Multiple Answers
Communicating	58	40
Controlling	25	17
Directing	23	16
Organizing	21	14
Planning	19	13
Total	146	100

Table 4. Why management is more difficult in small companies, according to presidents of small companies.

Reason	Number of Mentions	Percent of Total
Insufficient staff	16	40
Lack of time	12	30
Lack of specialization	11	28
Lack of EDP	1	2
Total	40	100

1785123

Table 5. Why management is more difficult in large companies, according to presidents of large companies.

Reason	Number of Mentions	Percent
More employees	26	46
Greater volume	17	30
Greater complexity	12	22
Greater departmentalization	1	2
Total	56	100

Table 6. Limitations imposed by small-size, according to presidents of small companies.

Limitations	Number of Mentions	Percent
Makes financing more difficult	63	23
Limits ability to develop new products	54	20
Makes it hard to attract specialist personnel	47	17
Limits ability to benefit from planning	43	16
Imposes restrictions on marketing	34	12
Limits risk-taking ability	34	12
Total	275	100

Table 7. Limitations imposed by large size, according to presidents of large companies.

Limitations	Number of Mentions	Percent
Limits flexibility, ability to change course quickly	20	27
Reduces ability to attract entrepreneurial personnel	11	15
Limits capacity to take risks	12	17
Complicates communications	9	12
Complicates long-range planning	4	6
Complicates personnel relations	4	6
Raises costs of product development	3	4
Imposes restrictions on marketing	3	4
Limits fulfillment of customer needs	2	2
Other (decision making, approval time, public image, etc.)	5	7
Total	73	100

Table 8. Areas in which large businesses have competitive superiority over small businesses.

Area	Small Company Presidents	Percent	Large Company Presidents	Percent
Sales coverage	45	20	77	21
Advertising	45	20	77	21
Pricing	42	18	22	6
Engineering/design	32	14	67	18
Distribution	31	14	78	21
Financing	9	4	8	2
Service	7	3	32	9
Other	17	7	8	2
Total	228	100	369	100

Table 9. Business activity or area in which small businesses have greater flexibility than large businesses.

Activity or Area	Small Company Presidents	Percent	Large Company Presidents	Percent
Customer service	86	21	51	17
Product changes	78	19	38	13
Production of special orders	78	19	61	20
Pricing	63	16	49	17
Budget changes	32	8	31	10
Production volume (output)	26	6	30	10
Employment (increasing or reducing staff)	25	6	25	8
Distribution	14	4	10	3
Decision making	5	1	5	2
Total	407	100	300	100

Table 10. Size of companies giving the toughest competition.

Size	Small Company Presidents	Percent	Large Company Presidents	Percent
Bigger companies	38	32	29	30
Companies of same size	30	26	19	20
Smaller companies	30	26	22	23
No pattern	19	16	26	27
Total	117	100	96	100

Table 11. Future scope of formal, detailed long-range plans.

Scope	In Small Companies	Percent	In Large Companies	Percent
5 to 10 years	3	5	3	3
5 years	26	45	55	64
3 years	15	26	11	13
1 year	8	14	4	5
18 months to 2 years	6	10	3	3
6 months	—	—	1	1
None	—	—	9	11
Total	58	100	86	100

Table 12. Major market changes affecting businesses in the past five years.

Nature of Change	Small Company Presidents	Percent	Large Company Presidents	Percent
New competition	55	37	55	38
Other products	41	28	31	22
Buying habits	28	19	34	24
Population shifts	6	4	5	4
None	4	3	—	—
Distribution costs	3	2	—	—
Defense spending	2	1	2	1
Foreign imports	2	1	4	3
Mergers	1	0.5	3	2
Technology	—	—	3	2
Pricing	—	—	2	1
Other (declining prices, government regulations, mortgage money, health factors, etc.)	7	4.5	3	3
Total	149	100	142	100

Table 13. Steps taken to anticipate market changes.

Steps Taken	In Small Companies	Percent	In Large Companies	Percent
New products/R&D	23	43	19	35
Market analysis and research	7	13	17	31
Long-range planning	—	—	6	11
Reliance on traditional measures	5	10	—	—
Sharpened buying	4	8	—	—
Failure to anticipate changes	—	—	3	5
Budgeting/cost reduction	—	—	3	5
Improved selling	2	4	—	—
Changes in prices	2	4	2	4
Increase in production	2	4	—	—
Improvement in planning	2	4	—	—
Mergers/acquisitions	—	—	2	4
Other (outlets, etc.)	5	10	3	5
Total	52	100	55	100

Table 14. Management tools in small and large companies.

Tool	Number of Mentions in Small Companies	Percent	Number of Mentions in Large Companies	Percent
Regular operating reports	84	18	83	15
Organization charts	71	15	81	15
Job descriptions	71	15	78	14
Standard policies	62	13	69	13
Standard procedures	61	13	75	14
Objectives	49	10.5	57	10
Long-range plans	44	9	58	10
Organization manuals	26	6	49	8
Other	2	0.5	5	1
Total	470	100	555	100

Table 15. Policy coverage.

Policy Coverage	In Small Companies	Percent	In Large Companies	Percent
Covers most areas	37	48	35	40
Covers personnel practices only	29	37	23	27
Covers all major areas	7	9	21	24
Other (supervisory, pricing, credit, accounting, sales, purchasing)	5	6	8	9
Total	78	100	87	100

Table 16. Current status of operating policies.

Status of Operating Policies	Small Companies	Percent	Large Companies	Percent
All up to date	29	40	35	47
Some up to date	40	55	34	46
Generally out of date	4	5	5	7
Total	73	100	74	100

Table 17. Extent to which policies are communicated.

Extent	Small Companies	Percent	Large Companies	Percent
Widely circulated	25	53	37	82
Poorly circulated	22	47	8	18
Total	47	100	45	100

Table 18. Uses for which accounting systems are adequate.

System	In Small Companies	Percent	In Large Companies	Percent
Pricing	85	21	70	18
Product costing	81	20	72	19
Make-or-buy decisions	66	16	57	15
Fixed asset investments	65	16	76	20
Profitability by product, customer, territory	60	14	48	13
Measuring management performance	54	13	57	15
Total	411	100	380	100

Table 19. Period covered by regular cash forecasts.

Period Covered	In Small Companies	Percent	In Large Companies	Percent
Daily	6	3	20	7.3
Weekly	4	2	2	0.7
Monthly	39	23	65	23
Quarterly	29	17	49	18
Semiannually	13	8	19	7
Annually	49	29	68	25
Every 3 years	12	7	14	5
Every 5 years	8	5	40	14
No cash forecasts made	11	6	–	–
Total	171	100	277	100

Table 20. Expenses identified and budgeted.

Item	In Small Companies	Percent	In Large Companies	Percent
Capital expenditures	78	16	88	15
Advertising	77	16	88	15
Sales	73	15	86	15
Administration	72	15	84	14.5
Factory	66	14	83	14
Purchases	62	13	68	12
R&D	53	11	81	14
Other (recruitment, service)	–	–	3	0.5
Total	481	100	581	100

Table 21. Percentages of sales that it costs to process data (including salaries) on punched cards or computer systems.

Percentage of Sales	In Small Companies	Percent	In Large Companies	Percent
Less than 1%	12	33	39	72
1%	10	28	6	11
1 to 2%	6	16	6	11
2 to 3%	4	11	3	6
5%	2	6	–	–
Over 5%	2	6	–	–
Total	36	100	54	100

Table 22. Kinds of systems used in inventory reporting.

System	In Small Companies	Percent	In Large Companies	Percent
Manual	63	54	73	58
Machine	26	23	29	23
Computer	26	23	23	19
Total	115	100	125	100

Table 23. Does inventory reporting system highlight fast- and slow-moving items?

	In Small Companies	Percent	In Large Companies	Percent
Yes	72	76	79	94
No	23	24	5	6
Total	95	100	84	100

Table 24. Frequency of review of approved supplier lists.

	In Small Companies	Percent	In Large Companies	Percent
Constantly	28	47	14	25
Monthly	3	5	—	—
Quarterly	2	3	5	9
Semiannually	7	12	6	11
Annually	20	33	27	48
Irregularly	—	—	4	7
Total	60	100	56	100

Table 25. Do small companies need to be as formally structured as large?

	No	Percent	Yes	Percent	Total	Percent
Small company presidents	78	62	25	36	103	53
Large company presidents	47	38	45	64	92	47
Total	125	100	70	100	195	100

Table 26. Reasons why small companies need not be formally structured.

Reasons Given	According to Small Company Presidents	Percent	According to Large Company Presidents	Percent
Closer contact with people	18	36	10	21
Executives wear many hats	13	26	7	15
More direct communication	7	14	14	30
More informal relationships	5	10	14	30
Other (less need for specialization, etc.)	7	14	2	4
Total	50	100	47	100

Table 27. Number of organization levels from president to line worker.

Number of Levels	In Small Companies	Percent	In Large Companies	Percent
1 level	4	4	—	—
2 levels	23	23	4	5
3 levels	38	37	9	11
4 levels	23	23	15	18
5 levels	10	10	24	29
6 levels	2	2	17	20
7 levels	1	1	8	10
More than 7 levels	—	—	6	7
Total	101	100	83	100

Table 28. Sources of managers, department heads, specialists.

Sources	In Small Companies	Percent	In Large Companies	Percent
Within the company	75	38	85	52
Random sources	53	26	24	15
Larger companies	29	14	15	9
Professional recruiters	22	11	20	12
Family	9	4	—	—
Smaller companies	8	4	8	5
Similar-size companies	—	—	11	7
Other	6	3	—	—
Total	202	100	163	100

Table 29. Activities staffed on a full-time basis.

Activities	In Small Companies	Percent	In Large Companies	Percent
Product development	66	30	78	19
Administration	51	23	70	17
Systems and procedures	35	16	75	18
Market research	22	10	73	18
Organization planning	13	6	44	11
Corporate development	12	5	48	12
Economic research	3	1	18	5
None	19	9	—	—
Total	221	100	406	100

Table 30. Areas in which shortages of competent people exist.

Area	In Small Companies	Percent	In Large Companies	Percent
Engineering	50	29	47	26
Manufacturing	41	24	25	14
Technical specialists	33	19	34	19
Marketing	31	18	33	18
Finance	9	6	25	14
Administration	4	2	7	4
Sales	2	1	2	1
EDP	–	–	4	2
Other	2	1	3	2
Total	172	100	180	100

Table 31. Areas in which supplemental personnel are used.

Area	In Small Companies	Percent	In Large Companies	Percent
Engineering	17	23	20	26
Plant and clerical workers	12	17	4	5
Technical (product development, packaging, etc.)	10	14	7	9
Finance	9	13	6	8
Marketing	8	11	8	10
Manufacturing	5	7	7	9
General management	4	5	4	5
Personnel	2	3	9	12
Other (EDP, systems)	5	7	12	16
Total	72	100	77	100

Table 32. Percent of college graduates in managerial/professional staff.

College Graduates on Staff	In Small Companies	Percent	In Large Companies	Percent
Under 30%	34	34	5	6
30 to 49%	13	13	4	5
50 to 74%	21	21	16	20
75 to 100%	33	32	55	69
Total	101	100	80	100

Table 33. Incidence of performance appraisal systems.

	In Small Companies	Percent	In Large Companies	Percent
Have an appraisal system	71	67	75	82
Do not have a system	35	33	16	18
Total	106	100	91	100

Table 34. Prevalence of management development programs.

	Small Companies	Percent	Large Companies	Percent
Have a development program	26	25	45	50
Do not have a program	79	75	45	50
Total	105	100	90	100

Table 35. Advantages large companies are thought to have in recruitment.

	Number of Companies	Percent
More chance of advancement	31	21
Company reputation (prestige)	31	21
Better fringe benefits	24	16.5
More job security	24	16.5
Higher pay	15	10
Better recruiting programs	15	10
Better training programs	4	3
Opportunity to specialize	2	1.3
Better use of capabilities	1	0.7
Total	147	100

Table 36. Destination of departing salaried employees.

	From Small Companies	Percent	From Large Companies	Percent
To larger companies	35	50	27	30
To companies of same size	15	21	17	19
To smaller companies	8	11	29	32
Don't know or no pattern	13	18	17	19
Total	71	100	90	100

Table 37. Why salaried employees leave.

Reasons	Small Companies	Percent	Large Companies	Percent
For more money	56	56	64	47
For more responsibility	20	20	41	30
For more security	7	7	5	3
For prestige	6	6	11	8
To establish own business	2	2	—	—
Other reasons	9	9	16	12
Total	100	100	137	100

Table 38. R&D expenditures as a percentage of sales.

Percentage	In Small Companies	Percent	In Large Companies	Percent
Less than 1%	20	26	16	21
1 to 1½%	15	19	17	23
2 to 3%	19	25	21	28
4 to 6%	12	16	13	17
Over 6%	11	14	8	11
Total	77	100	75	100

Table 39. Executive activities impaired by lack of time.

Activities	In Small Companies	Percent	In Large Companies	Percent
Planning	31	32	34	41
Personnel relations	15	15	9	11
Sales and marketing	14	14	—	—
Communications, contacts, visits	6	6	8	10
Thinking	6	6	9	11
Management development	5	5	4	5
Reading	5	5	8	10
Other activities (budgeting, controlling, production, product development, organization development)	13	13	8	10
None	4	4	2	2
Total	99	100	82	100

Table 40. *Length of typical working day of top executives.*

	In Small Companies	*Percent*	*In Large Companies*	*Percent*
Seven hours	5	5	—	—
Eight hours	19	18	21	24
Nine hours	40	38	38	44
Ten hours	28	27	20	23
Over ten hours	13	12	8	9
Total	105	100	87	100

Table 41. *Span of control of presidents.*

Number of People	*In Small Companies*	*Percent*	*In Large Companies*	*Percent*
3 people or fewer	9	9	7	8
4 people	17	18	7	8
5 people	19	19	11	12
6 people	12	12	12	13
7 people	19	19	10	12
8 people	9	9	16	17
9 to 10 people	5	5	16	17
11 people and over	9	9	12	13
Total	99	100	91	100

Table 42. *Length of time president had been in office at time of survey.*

Years in Office	*In Small Companies*	*Percent*	*In Large Companies*	*Percent*
1 year or less	2	2	24	27
1 to 5 years	31	30	41	46
6 to 10 years	16	16	11	13
11 to 20 years	34	33	7	8
Over 20 years	19	19	5	6
Total	102	100	88	100

Table 43. Profit before taxes to sales and to net worth in selected industries of companies of different size.

	SALES				SALES			
	250M but Less than 1MM	1MM but Less than 10MM	10MM but Less than 25MM	All Sizes	250M but Less than 1MM	1MM but Less than 10MM	10MM but Less than 25MM	All Sizes
	Profit Before Taxes to Sales (Percent)				Profit Before Taxes to Net Worth (Percent)			
Manufacturers								
Industrial chemicals	3.6	5.4	9.0	7.4	16.7	16.7	20.1	17.8
Electronic components and accessories	1.1	1.2	2.8	2.1	10.9	7.4	11.1	9.4
Construction and mining machinery and equipment..	3.3	5.9	5.4	5.5	8.8	14.1	15.0	14.0
Pulp paper and paperboard	N/A	3.2	2.3	2.7	N/A	12.4	6.9	12.4
Motor vehicle parts and accessories	3.7	4.7	4.9	4.8	16.8	17.8	10.9	17.3
General industrial machinery and equipment	3.6	4.9	6.4	5.5	15.0	13.1	17.2	14.9
Fabricated structural steel	1.6	4.2	5.3	4.4	12.0	17.7	14.9	14.5
Wholesalers								
Hardware and paints	2.6	2.5	2.1	2.3	10.7	9.9	6.2	10.3
Heavy commercial and industrial machinery and equipment	2.2	3.3	3.5	3.2	10.4	15.0	19.4	13.3
Retailers								
Department stores	3.7	3.5	4.2	3.9	10.8	12.3	15.1	12.3
Groceries and meats	1.8	1.5	1.4	1.5	19.0	20.4	18.1	20.7
Road machinery and equipment	1.6	2.9	6.5	4.7	7.3	14.7	23.6	16.7

Percentages based on Financial Statements for fiscal years ending in 1970.
Source: Annual Statement Studies, 1971 Edition, Robert Morris Associates, Philadelphia, Pa.

Note: In most cases the companies in the $10 million to $25 million sales category had the highest profitability. Data are selected because there were few industry categories in which the largest sales category reported.

6200 1